P9-EMR-353

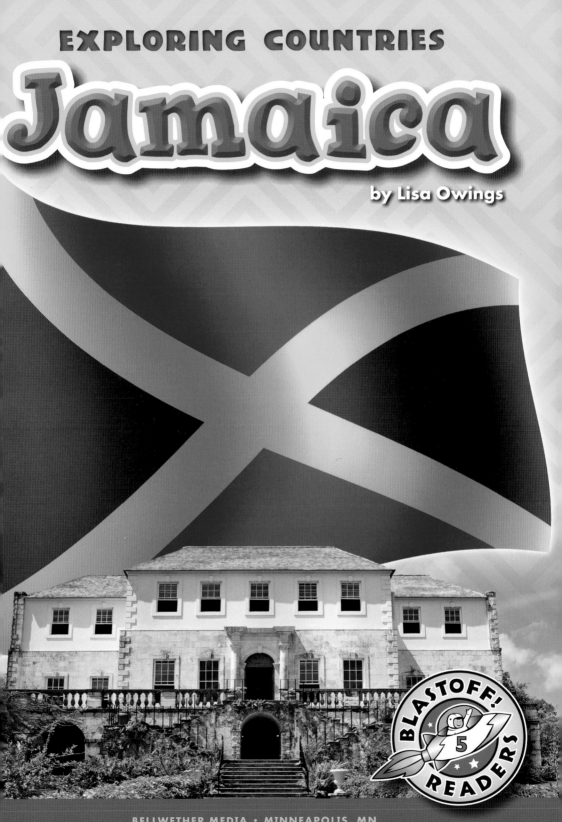

EXPLORING COUNTRIES

Jamaica

by Lisa Owings

BELLWETHER MEDIA • MINNEAPOLIS, MN

Note to Librarians, Teachers, and Parents:

Blastoff! Readers are carefully developed by literacy experts and combine standards-based content with developmentally appropriate text.

Level 1 provides the most support through repetition of high-frequency words, light text, predictable sentence patterns, and strong visual support.

Level 2 offers early readers a bit more challenge through varied simple sentences, increased text load, and less repetition of high-frequency words.

Level 3 advances early-fluent readers toward fluency through increased text and concept load, less reliance on visuals, longer sentences, and more literary language.

Level 4 builds reading stamina by providing more text per page, increased use of punctuation, greater variation in sentence patterns, and increasingly challenging vocabulary.

Level 5 encourages children to move from "learning to read" to "reading to learn" by providing even more text, varied writing styles, and less familiar topics.

Whichever book is right for your reader, Blastoff! Readers are the perfect books to build confidence and encourage a love of reading that will last a lifetime!

This edition first published in 2014 by Bellwether Media, Inc.

Library of Congress Cataloging-in-Publication Data

Owings, Lisa.
Jamaica / by Lisa Owings.
pages cm. – (Blastoff! Readers: Exploring Countries)
Summary: "Developed by literacy experts for students in grades three through seven, this book introduces young readers to the geography and culture of Jamaica"– Provided by publisher.
Includes bibliographical references and index.
ISBN 978-1-62617-067-4 (hardcover : alk. paper)
1. Jamaica–Juvenile literature. I. Title.
F1868.2.O95 2014
972.92–dc23

2013032870

Printed in the United States of America, North Mankato, MN.

Contents

Where Is Jamaica?

Did you know?
Jamaica is the third-largest island in the Caribbean after Cuba and Hispaniola. It is still smaller than the state of Connecticut.

Jamaica is an island country. It rises from the clear blue Caribbean Sea off the southeastern coast of North America. Jamaica's closest neighbor is Cuba to the north. Haiti and the Dominican Republic share the island of Hispaniola to the east. To the northwest are the tiny Cayman Islands.

Across a larger stretch of the Caribbean lies Central America to the west. There, the closest point of land to Jamaica is Cape Gracias a Dios on the border of Nicaragua and Honduras. Jamaica's closest neighbor to the south is Colombia in South America. Kingston is the island's capital. It was built along a natural **harbor** on Jamaica's southeastern coast.

Most of Jamaica is ridged with mountains covered in lush forests. The Blue Mountains in the east boast the tallest peaks. Lower mountains spread across the center of the island from east to west. In the northwest, **limestone** has **eroded** into a pattern of hills and pits. This region is known as Cockpit Country. The only flat land is found on the coast, where soft sand beaches meet clear ocean waves.

Rivers cascade from the mountains toward the sea. The longest are the Rio Minho, the Rio Cobre, and the Black River. Many rivers trickle into caves or rush over waterfalls before flowing into the Caribbean.

fun fact

Swirling storms called hurricanes often hit the island in summer and early fall.

Did you know?

Jamaica is warm year-round. The mountain air is cooler, and ocean breezes fan the coast. Rain comes in the spring and fall.

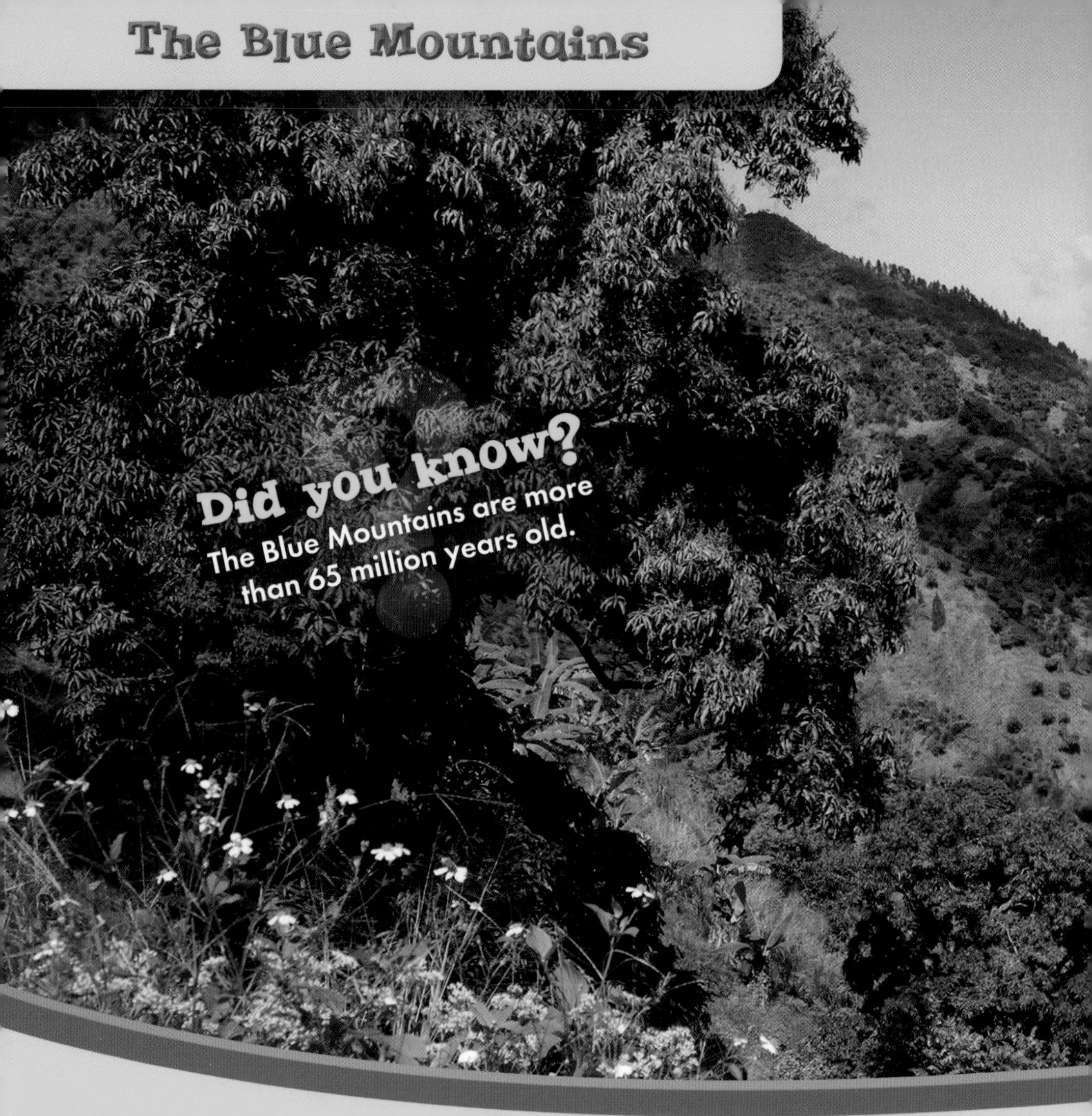

Did you know?
The Blue Mountains are more than 65 million years old.

High above Kingston rise the Blue Mountains. Their peaks stretch for nearly 30 miles (50 kilometers) through eastern Jamaica. Blue Mountain Peak is the island's highest point at 7,402 feet (2,256 meters). People often hike through the night to reach its **summit** at sunrise. From there, hikers can sometimes see Cuba along the northern **horizon**.

fun fact

Farmers grow coffee in the valleys of the Blue Mountains. Blue Mountain coffee is one of the best-tasting and most expensive coffees in the world.

From a distance, mists cloak the peaks in blue. Closer up, the mountains are green with **tropical** forests. Lacey ferns and colorful orchids give way to stalks of bamboo and large trees. Many of the plants are found nowhere else in the world. The Blue and John Crow Mountains National Park protects this rare landscape.

streamertail hummingbird

Many animals thrive in Jamaica's forests and warm waters. More than 200 kinds of birds flit through the island's treetops. The streamertail hummingbird was named for its long tail feathers. Bright green parrots and Jamaican todies are hard to spot against forest **canopies**. The country's few mammals include guinea pig-like hutias. Mongooses chase after rats and snakes. At night, bats swoop out of caves to feed.

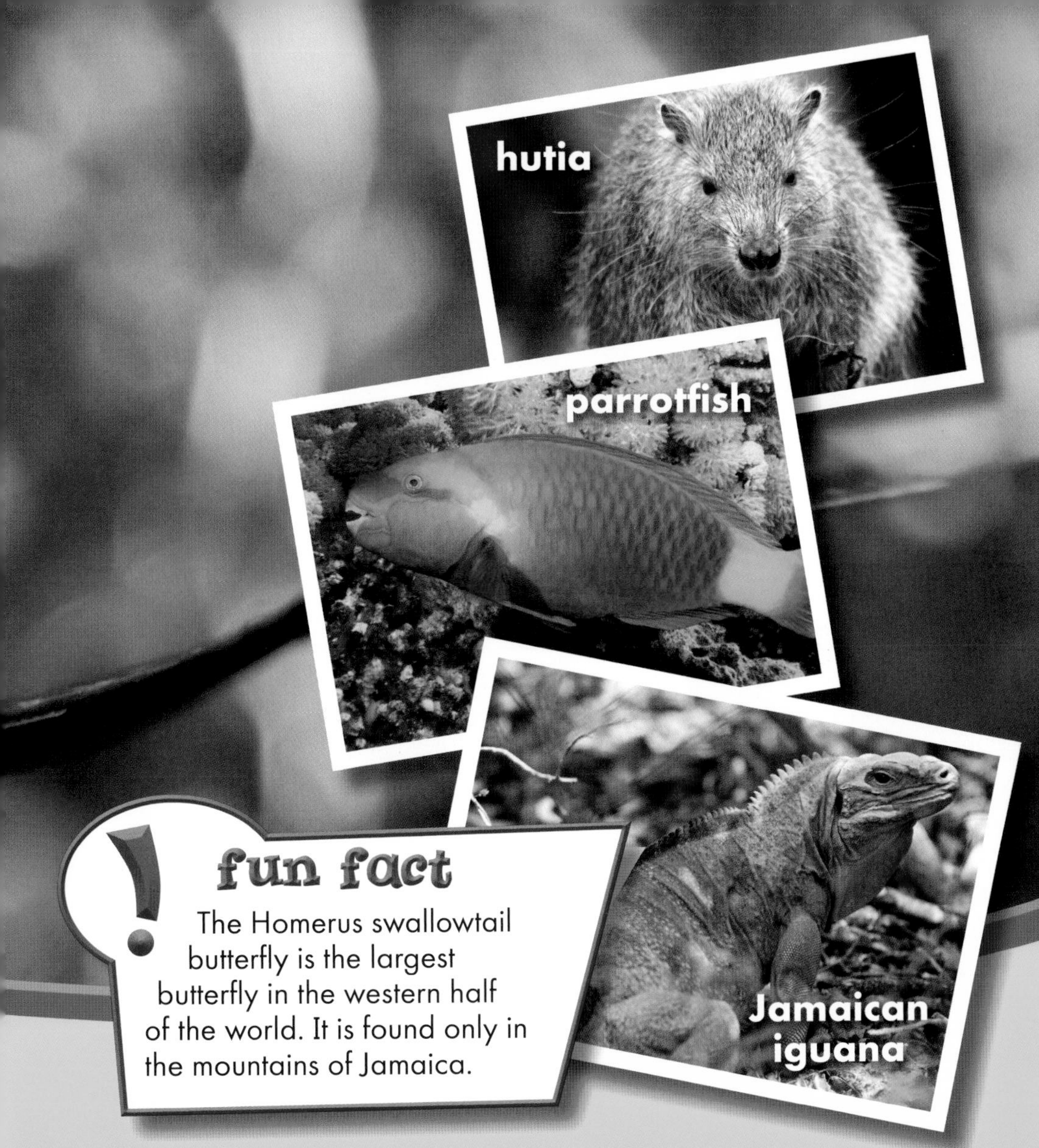

fun fact

The Homerus swallowtail butterfly is the largest butterfly in the western half of the world. It is found only in the mountains of Jamaica.

Large Jamaican iguanas are found in southern forests. Other reptiles include crocodiles that lurk in the island's rivers and wetlands. Manatees drift through rivers and shallow coastal waters. Rare sea turtles, bright parrotfish, and other sea creatures share the **coral reefs** surrounding the island.

Around 3 million people live in Jamaica. More than nine out of every ten Jamaicans have African **ancestors**. Many of these ancestors were brought to the island as **slaves** to work on large farms. Other Jamaicans have ancestors from Europe or Asia. Many come from mixed backgrounds. English is Jamaica's official language, but most Jamaicans speak a language called Patois. It is a mixture of English, Spanish, French, and African languages.

Jamaicans are known for being fun-loving and friendly. Their personalities come out in their colorful clothing, lively gestures, and playful sense of humor. They are proud of their nation's accomplishments and hope to continue to make Jamaica a better place.

Speak Jamaican Patois!

Patois	Meaning
wah gwann	hello/what's going on?
walk good	good-bye/take care
likkle more	see you later
irie	good/everything is great
feel no way	don't worry about it
mek wi nyam	let's eat
a weh yuh seh?	what did you say?
everyt'ing criss?	everything okay?
a wa?	what is it?
nah man!	forget about it!

Just over half of Jamaicans live in cities. The rest live in the countryside. Most have small houses or apartments. A few wealthy Jamaicans live in large mansions, but many people cannot afford a home at all. They build small shacks wherever they can find space. The contrast between wealthy and poor Jamaicans is a source of conflict and crime on the island.

Many Jamaicans travel by car. Others crowd onto buses or take taxis. Shopping takes place at large malls or small local shops. At home, children in Jamaica help with chores such as cooking and cleaning. Older children often help care for younger siblings while their parents are at work.

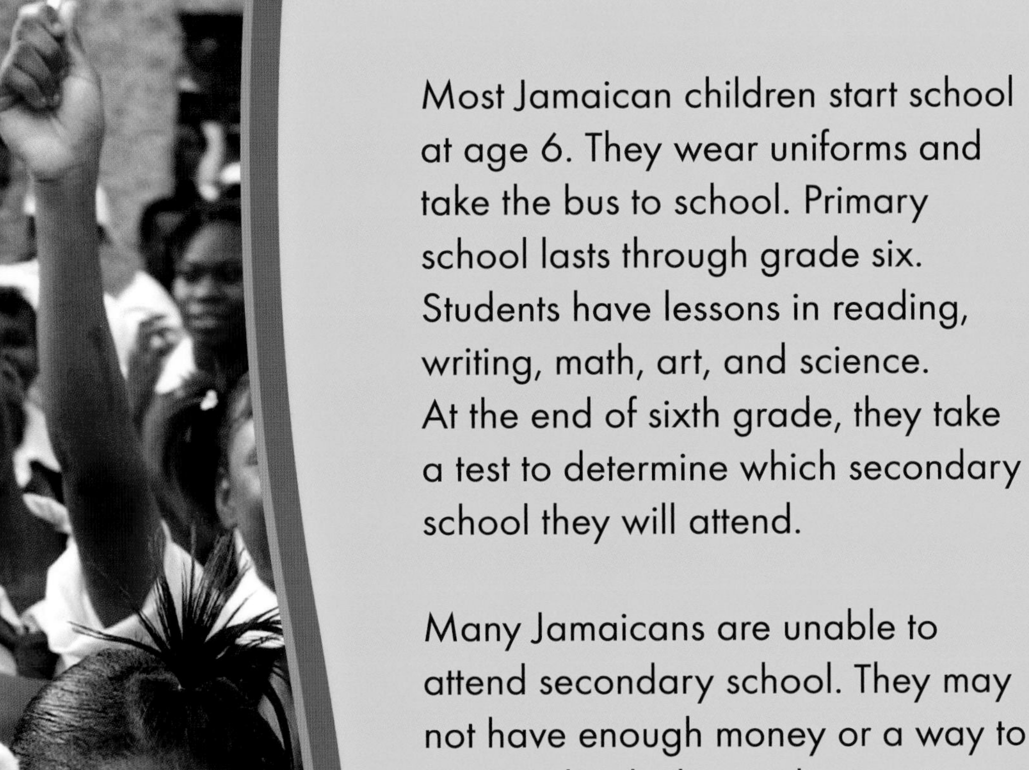

Most Jamaican children start school at age 6. They wear uniforms and take the bus to school. Primary school lasts through grade six. Students have lessons in reading, writing, math, art, and science. At the end of sixth grade, they take a test to determine which secondary school they will attend.

Many Jamaicans are unable to attend secondary school. They may not have enough money or a way to get to school. Those who continue take classes in math, science, language, and technology. Some graduates move on to schools that teach them specific jobs. Others apply to colleges or universities.

fun fact

Students in Jamaica have to be on their best behavior when in uniform. They can get in trouble for shouting or eating in public while wearing their school clothes.

Where People Work in Jamaica

manufacturing 19%

farming 17%

services 64%

Did you know?

Some of the waste from Jamaica's sugarcane harvest is used to make electricity and fuel.

Over half of Jamaicans work in **service jobs**. Many serve the nearly 2 million **tourists** who visit the island each year. They work at **resorts**, restaurants, and tourist attractions. Others work in banks, shops, and schools. Some Jamaicans make paintings, wood carvings, straw hats, and other crafts. They sell them at markets near tourist areas.

In the countryside, many farmers grow sugarcane. Factory workers turn the crop into sugar, molasses, and rum. Fruits such as bananas and coconuts are other important crops. Miners dig for rust-colored bauxite, which is turned into aluminum. Off the coasts, fishers cast their nets for lobsters, conches, and fish.

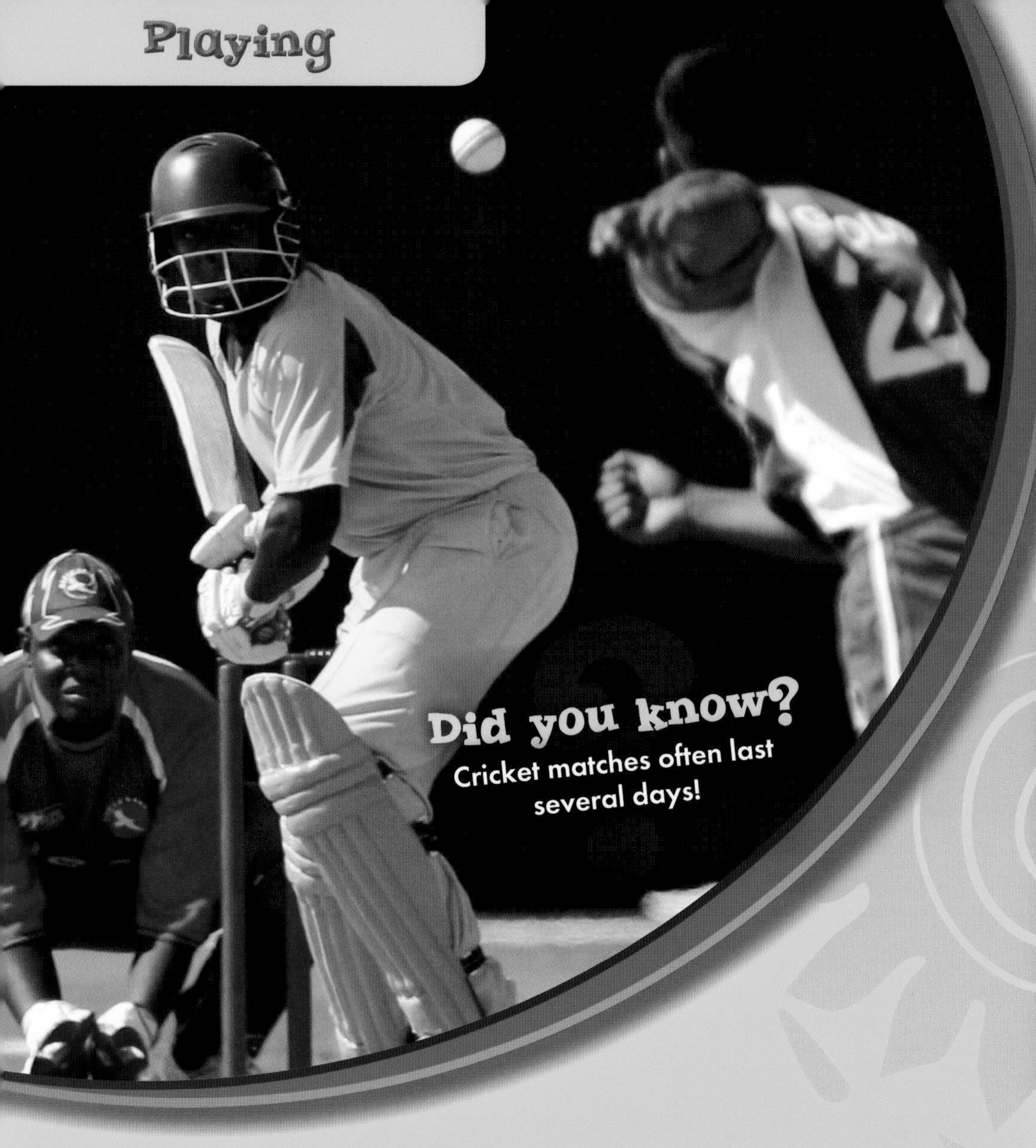

Did you know?
Cricket matches often last several days!

Jamaicans love spending time with family and friends. They go to beaches to relax or swim. Families enjoy vacations at the island's many resorts. Young Jamaicans like to go dancing with friends. Going to movies and plays are other common activities.

Jamaicans of all ages enjoy sports and games. Cricket is a popular sport. Similar to baseball, players score by hitting balls with wooden bats and running. Soccer fans cheer on the national team, the Reggae Boyz. Girls especially like to play netball, a game similar to basketball. Off the court, Jamaicans gather to play dominoes, jacks, or dice games.

fun fact

Track and field is Jamaica's strongest Olympic sport. National hero and gold-medal sprinter Usain Bolt is widely known as the fastest man in the world.

Usain Bolt

Flavorful, spicy food is Jamaica's specialty. Ackee and saltfish is a classic breakfast. Salted cod is served with a fruit that looks and tastes similar to scrambled eggs. Jerk meat is another favorite meal. Pork or chicken is coated in spices and then barbecued to give it a smoky flavor. Rice and beans or fried plantains are often served on the side.

Busy Jamaicans can grab a patty, or meat-filled pastry, on the go. Tropical fruits such as coconuts and mangoes are other tasty treats. On a hot day, many Jamaicans can be spotted eating flavored shaved ice called sky juice. Families gather on Sundays to eat a large meal together.

fun fact

Goat meat is commonly eaten in Jamaica. It is used in curries, stews, and soups.

goat curry

ackee and saltfish

Christmas is one of the biggest holidays in Jamaica. Families usually go to church and spend time with friends and relatives. They feast on ham, Christmas cake, and a drink made from sorrel flowers. Children can stay up all night on Christmas Eve. They have fun shopping at the carnival-like Grand Markets that spring up all over the island.

In spring, brightly costumed dancers and parade floats fill the streets during *Carnival*. On Easter, some families attend church. Others visit with family and friends. Independence Day on August 6 marks Jamaica's independence from Britain. Thousands head to Kingston's National Stadium for a parade, music, speeches, and fireworks.

Independence Day

Did you know?

Emancipation Day on August 1 marks the day slavery ended in Jamaica. Church bells and beating drums sound at midnight.

The Rastafari movement is a religion for a small group of Jamaicans. Rastas **worship** former Ethiopian emperor Halie Selassie I. They believe Selassie will someday return them to Africa, which they see as their true home. Many Rastas wear their hair in long **dreadlocks**. They also wear the red, green, and gold colors of the Ethiopian flag.

Around the 1970s, reggae music became tied to the Rastafari movement. Reggae combines Jamaican sounds with rock and soul. It has a laid-back **tempo** with a strong rhythm. Bob Marley was the most famous Jamaican reggae artist. He often sang about his Rastafarian beliefs. Marley's music became popular across the globe. Through rastas and reggae, this small country made a big impression on the world.

Halie Selassie I

Bob Marley

Did you know?
Before Selassie became emperor, he was called Prince Tafari, or Ras Tafari in the Ethiopian language. The Rastafari movement was named after him.

Fast Facts About Jamaica

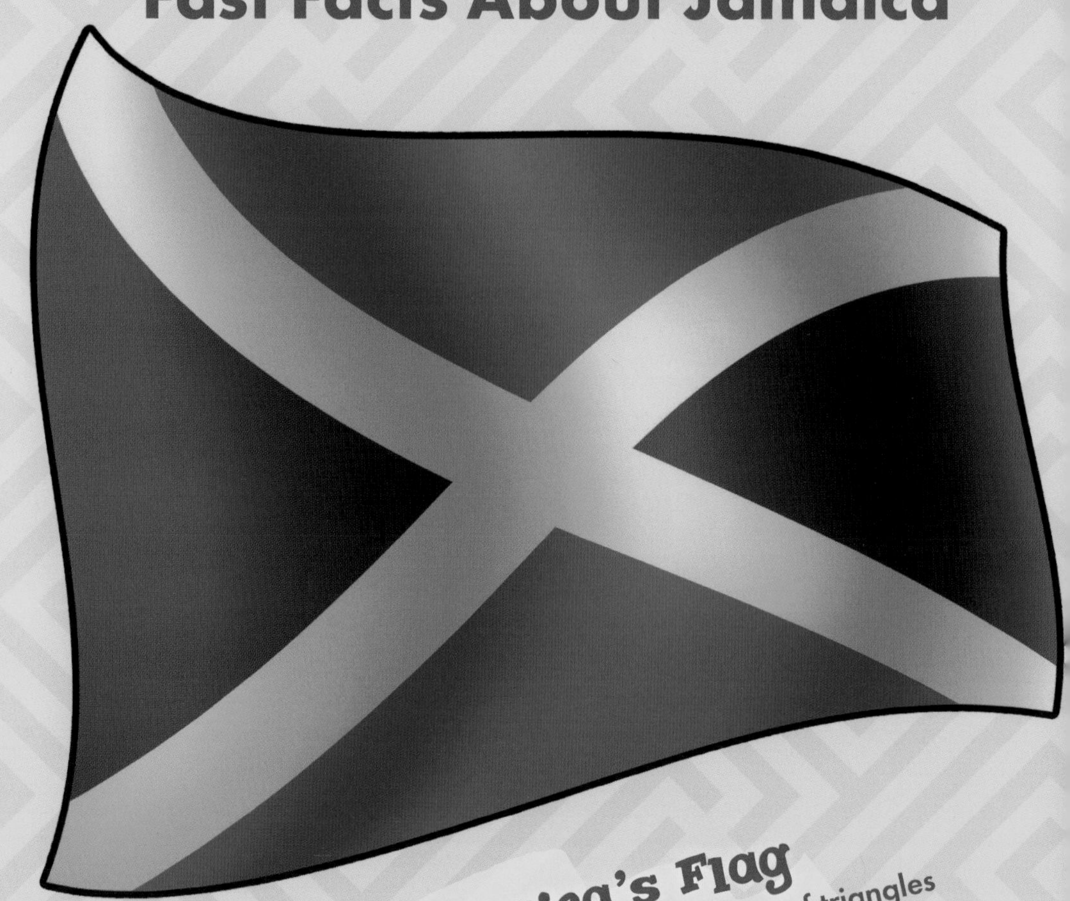

Jamaica's Flag

The Jamaican flag features two pairs of triangles divided by a yellow X. The top and bottom triangles are green to represent farming and hope for the future. The triangles on the left and right are black. They symbolize the nation's struggles. The yellow represents Jamaica's sunshine and natural resources. This flag was adopted on August 6, 1962.

Official Name:	Jamaica
Area:	4,244 square miles (10,992 square kilometers); Jamaica is the 168th largest country in the world.

Capital City:	Kingston
Important Cities:	Spanish Town, Portmore, Montego Bay
Population:	2,909,714 (July 2013)
Official Language:	English
National Holiday:	Independence Day (August 6)
Religions:	Christian (65.1%), other (14.2%), none (20.7%)
Major Industries:	tourism, mining, farming, fishing
Natural Resources:	bauxite, gypsum, limestone, iron ore, silica sand
Manufactured Products:	aluminum, sugar, rum, chemicals, clothing, cement
Farm Products:	sugarcane, coffee beans, bananas, citrus, yams, ackee, allspice, goats
Unit of Money:	Jamaican dollar; the Jamaican dollar is divided into 100 cents.

Glossary

ancestors—relatives who lived long ago

canopies—thick coverings of leafy branches formed by the tops of trees

coral reefs—structures made of coral that usually grow in shallow seawater

dreadlocks—hair worn in matted ropes or braids

eroded—slowly worn away by water or wind

harbor—a place where ships can dock

horizon—the line where the earth or water meets the sky

limestone—a type of rock formed from shells and coral over millions of years

resorts—vacation spots that offer entertainment, recreation, and relaxation

service jobs—jobs that perform tasks for people or businesses

slaves—people who were owned as property and forced to work for no pay

summit—the highest point of something

tempo—the speed of a piece of music

tourists—people who travel to visit another place

tropical—part of the tropics; the tropics is a hot, rainy region near the equator.

worship—to show love and devotion to someone or something, usually a god

To Learn More

AT THE LIBRARY

Capek, Michael. *Jamaica*. Minneapolis, Minn.: Lerner Publications Company, 2010.

Medina, Tony. *I and I: Bob Marley*. New York, N.Y.: Lee & Low Books, 2009.

Savage, Jeff. *Usain Bolt*. Minneapolis, Minn.: Lerner Publications Company, 2013.

ON THE WEB

Learning more about Jamaica is as easy as 1, 2, 3.

1. Go to www.factsurfer.com.
2. Enter "Jamaica" into the search box.
3. Click the "Surf" button and you will see a list of related Web sites.

With factsurfer.com, finding more information is just a click away.

Index

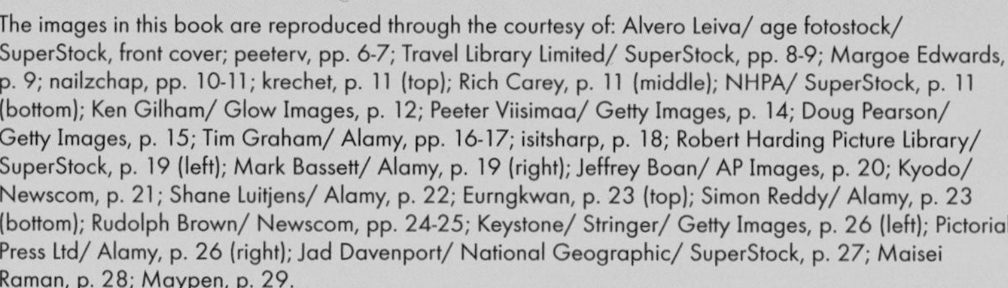

The images in this book are reproduced through the courtesy of: Alvero Leiva/ age fotostock/ SuperStock, front cover; peeterv, pp. 6-7; Travel Library Limited/ SuperStock, pp. 8-9; Margoe Edwards, p. 9; nailzchap, pp. 10-11; krechet, p. 11 (top); Rich Carey, p. 11 (middle); NHPA/ SuperStock, p. 11 (bottom); Ken Gilham/ Glow Images, p. 12; Peeter Viisimaa/ Getty Images, p. 14; Doug Pearson/ Getty Images, p. 15; Tim Graham/ Alamy, pp. 16-17; isitsharp, p. 18; Robert Harding Picture Library/ SuperStock, p. 19 (left); Mark Bassett/ Alamy, p. 19 (right); Jeffrey Boan/ AP Images, p. 20; Kyodo/ Newscom, p. 21; Shane Luitjens/ Alamy, p. 22; Eurngkwan, p. 23 (top); Simon Reddy/ Alamy, p. 23 (bottom); Rudolph Brown/ Newscom, pp. 24-25; Keystone/ Stringer/ Getty Images, p. 26 (left); Pictorial Press Ltd/ Alamy, p. 26 (right); Jad Davenport/ National Geographic/ SuperStock, p. 27; Maisei Raman, p. 28; Maypen, p. 29.